Sanctuary of the Soul:

Poems
of
Anguish,
Healing, Hope,
Comfort, and Celebration

Alice M. Carleton

Mystic Publishers

Henderson, Nevada

2009

To all
who read :
Love and Peace

Kindest Regards
Alis Carlton

E:Mail: wacalice@aol.com

Anna Lillian Wareing
My Beloved Teacher and Friend
1912-2009

Mrs. Wareing was my 3rd grade teacher. She was magic, and touched and enriched the lives of everyone who met her. She had amazing vitality and energy and loved life. She learned to play the piano by ear and was playing by age 4, and also played for silent films. She called me a "fairy-child" and when I told her she had some fairy-child in her character also, she said: "Let's just keep on doing that—to the grave!" In her 90s 'she was still performing in plays, and in one of them, dressed as Willie Nelson. What a legacy she left. We were kindred spirits, and I will miss her for the rest of my life.

Acknowledgments

I thank my sister, Karen Boutin for the cover image. I also thank Kathie Lesich for her graphic design in assembling the cover.

Table of Contents

Table of Contents
(continued)

Sanctuary of the Soul

Maine Whispers

Maine whispers low
Inviting you
For we have things to show
We want you to know
Sometimes in a misting cascading waterfall
You may hear its' call
At the roaring of the ocean door
One cannot ask for more
In a whippoorwill song
Stay and listen—linger long
Weeping willows in the sun
Never done
Swaying in their beauty for all to see
The sensitive, quaking, quivering aspen
Asking
We missed you, where have you been?
Cheerful warm inviting people
New England church steeples
Winking lighthouses in the fog at night
Sailor's saviors and delight
Millions of stars strewn in the darkness
Your soul to bless

Whales breaching the ocean surface while
We watch in awe
Diving with ease without one flaw
Nature singing
Sea birds winging
Deep dark forests elegantly standing
The silver silence reigns
Their beauty king
Stay awhile
Drink in the ecstasy
Just be
Powerful eagles and peregrine
Preening their feathers to a brilliant sheen
It's Christmas and the Fourth of July
Such sorrow to have to say goodbye
One does not breathe there
One drinks the air
Brilliant glorious flashing autumn leaves
For this one grieves
Butterflies and buttercups and dragonflies
A baby robins' sleepy sighs
A pink and purple dawn unfolds in panoramic
view
Asking you and inviting you to look at me
This is for you
Loveliness and mystery

Nature at its best
Lie down and rest
The eternal tide
Rising and falling, turning over
The mournful sound of a buoy
Mysterious you cannot see
Diamonds in the waves
Craggy granite darkened caves
Do not miss it
Embrace and "kiss" it
When she goes to bed
She lies in stars and inky night
To everyone's delight
In her black velvet gown she lies down
Taking of her shining crown
Resting on her soft and supple arms
Resting on her myriad charms
Sometimes in her negligee
The aurora borealis
Her private palace
Like an elegant beautiful woman
She never grows old
Every day brings renewal
In her glory to behold
Her passionate nature never cold

In deepest Winter
Eternally warm
She wraps you in her arms
Irresistible charms
You never will be cold
Sanctuary at last
All else is past
Peace be still
Allow
Your soul to fill

The Wake

I sit alone at the wake
It comes and goes, the ache
I wear black on the inside
It appears as if I've never cried
I wonder who it is that died
There are no other mourners at the gathering
No eulogies or songs to sing
The casket contains and is closed to symbolize
Needs unmet
There are no flowers
The death of hope of saddest hours
This is a wake of solitude
A mourner's fugue
No pictures surround the dead
No one remembering
This is what she said
There are picture frames
Devoid of photos, which should be there
Of a life where nothing was ever shared
Because the "murderer" never cared
The lights are low
The funeral director quietly asks

Are you ready to go?
To take the journey
The burden to lie it down
Upon the hardened ground
All without one sound
The silent dark procession of the soul
The journey to be whole
From grief relief
You must say goodbye I know
You didn't want to die
Sign the guest book and take one last look
The funeral was over many years ago
The tears, the pain and anguish is something
You too well do know
The silent vigil you still keep
While wandering in your sleep
I must sit a little longer
And when I am ready I will go
There is no one to stand with you at the grave
There was nothing that could be saved`
Isn't it ironic that they call it
A wake (awake)

The Night bird's Song

The night bird
Not often heard
Sings her sweetest song
Just before the glorious dawn
That song resonates
While the Universe anticipates
And lingers in the air
It says I care, your pain I will share
As her last sweet notes drift away
There dawns the day
Her concert done
She greets the sun
And flies away
Announces the day has just begun
She returns at night in joyful flight
To her concert hall
Little being so delicate and small
At the precise moment
Her timing instinctive
Exquisite
The darkened forest listens
Quietly waiting to hear it

What will she sing
The music—to escort the dawn
To gently bring
All nature holds its' breath
Waits to resonate with her
The ocean's roar
A kitten's purr
Stars close their eyes and wink their last
Tonight is past
The moon resigns and folds her silvery wings
Takes the mysterious journey
To the other side of the world
The symphony of the soul
Is the one
Which only the heart
Can see

Fragile Things

Gossamer fairy wings
Dragonfly's wings
The sound of a newborn robin
Beginning to sing
Glittery delicate
Crystal things
Rain on growing things
Around the moon
Clouds of rings
People's minds
In a world sometimes blind, unkind
Life and desperation, struggle and strife
Love is all that matters
Although all around everything may shatter
Fragile things
Beauty which moonbeams bring
Freedom's wings
Freedom sings
Freedom is a growing thing
Freedom rings

Oh What a Feeling

Oh what a feeling
Dancing on the ceiling
Joy bells are pealing
Celebrating healing
An angel bows low and touches the ground
You have been found
You are unbound
The Universe sings with me
You are who you are meant to be
Flying free
The music of the spheres
Humming no more fears
Planets aligning
No more sighing
Your voice is heard
Now sing
Back to yourself you now bring
Birds are singing
Freedom found winging
The ocean pounds
A concert of powerful sounds
It is Christmas and the Fourth of July

You refused to "die"
Fireworks
No more hurts
Throw confetti
For she is ready
Soft and misty rain
Gentles away the pain
Christening pink champagne
Against the bow of a ship
The maiden voyage
A magical new trip
Throw the ticker-tape parade
For her history has been made
The forest sighs
Lightening stitches out in fire
Across the skies
She flies!

Moonflight

I flew to the moon last night
Guided by shafts of shining light
By love held so close and so tight
Then I flew to the stars
And piqued my curiosity in a visit with Venus and
Mars
I danced in diaphanous gauzy silk
Stopped by the milky way for a glass of celestial milk
My grand jetes were weightless
I was addicted to the dance I must confess
My silver slippers sparkled while sparks snapped and
fire crackled
While I danced to the Tarantella
Bellisima..Bella!
I listened to the music of the spheres
Suspended were time and tears
I leaped so high that I touched the roof of the sky
Brushed an angels wing
She said, welcome to the heavenly choir...we'd like to
invite you to sing.
Their invitation was engraved on heavenly calligraphy
A silver cloud wrapped in a scroll
I feared it to unroll

King David's harpsichord brushed an exquisite other-
worldly sound
It slipped into my hands with beauty so unbound
The angels closed their eyes and folded magnificent
wings
In reverence and as one they said
We await your joy to ring

Inauguration (2009) Poem

Prayer of Hope

Hope is a fragile thing
Which flies on delicate wing
It is the flutter of a beating heart
For renewal
Of which we are all a part
We join our hands and hearts
The newness of that start
We sing in joy as one
The work which must be done
"O beautiful for spacious skies"
For hope which onward and upward flies
In coldest winter
The hope of spring is always sure
Our nation shall forever endure
After the rain...the rainbow
The promise of what we know
Together we pray and sing
Together we let freedom ring
We say to fear

You have no business here
Our message to the world
The freedom banner gloriously unfurled
Stitched in lightening and fiercest fire
To this our nation does aspire
Throw a ticker-tape parade
For history has been made
Yes President Obama you can
Yes we can

When a Child is Born

The angels throw a celestial celebration
Pink champagne and powdered angel wings they
bring
They throw a rainbow into the sky
And sing a heavenly lullaby
Their harps are resonating
The strings which joy to all who hear do bring
They dance in exquisite loveliness
Bowing and graceful as lilies of the field
From heaven we expect nothing less
Their celebration and laughter fill the Universe
Stars gleam brighter
Souls are lighter
They choose a guardian for the newborn
Gabriel is present and blows his horn
New stars are flung into the sky
Angel "confetti" from on high
Written on a scroll in heavenly calligraphy
A birth certificate penned in silver—lovely memory
Of all you are meant to be
The guardian angel whispers in the newborn's ear
For your life I will always be near
Call and I...will always hear

Just What to Do

The flowers know just when to fold their petals
into sleep
The ocean knows just when to roll from depths
unknown
With power mysterious and deep
Foliage knows when to shake off their "clothes"
Waiting for the wind which blows
Trees left bare
Do not have a care
Waiting for the Spring all dressed in lovely green
Showing off their freshening sheen
The weeping willow sweeps on in
Birds alight upon its branches
A rest on fragrant pillow
Trailing tendrils in the stream
Beautiful, extravagant
Showy..as if in a dream
If a weed can push through concrete
What have we to fear
The challenges we meet
Bees buzz
Caterpillars fuzz
Swans glide

Chipmunks play seek and hide
Whenever a new life is born
Angels know just when to sing
Their harps are brushed with heavenly exquisite
Delicate wing
A celestial chord is touched and resonating
Heaven at its best is celebrating
When a child is born—so is hope
Looking through life's telescope
At mysteries and stars and planets so far away
To try and get a glimpse
Who will God's precious child grow up to be some-
day
In Winter rivers of ice just know when to break
But the ice around the heart carries and ache
Which only love can start
The iridescent hummingbird
Rarely seen or heard
Finds the nectar and searches near and far
The heart goes where it will
Its mission to fulfill
Exquisite violins pleading, bleeding, weep and
speak
Awakening a soul too long asleep
The wind knows just when to blow

We cannot see it come or go
The sun knows just when to shine
Illumined by the Great Divine
The moon knows just when to glow
Turning lights down so soft and low
The music of the Universe encompasses about
If we are quiet we will hear it
There is no doubt
Little fawns on shaky feet
Their mothers teaching them
Whispering in a silky ear
I am right here, no fear
The desert awakens all so miraculously
We should all "bloom"
Wake up and see
All nature knows just what to do
Would that we as humans
Knew that too

I Understand

Great drops of blood
The Flood
The Hebrews enslaved in brick and straw and mud
Those who are in peril out on the sea
That could be you, it could be me
Joseph sold into slavery
Wandering in the wilderness for forty years
The tears
The fiery furnace
Coals which burn and hiss
The question of all humanity
Their cry
The how...the why
Why did this have to be
The wounds
The loss
The cross
I understand the agony of
"Why has thou forsaken me?"

Loneliness

The loneliness settles in
Rushes in
And crushes in
It never asks
Where have you been?
A familiar companion from
The deepest cave
The darkest canyon
At those times I cannot see
The light
Shining from the lighthouse
To keep me from
The jagged rocks
It smiles
It mocks
It never asks
How was your day?
I missed you..sit down
And talk to me
I'd like to hear what you have to say
Please stay
Shadows on the wall

There is no one here
At all
We cast our dirge
Our pall
But every day I arise again
Wondering
How long and when
It does not want you to leave
Wants only
For you to grieve
A cruel taskmaster at its own pace
An emotional race
Sometimes it lets you go for awhile
But returns
With its evil smile
I will never give you what you need
As long as I am with you in word and thought and
deed
I will leave your heart to bleed
I care nothing for your need
The broken chord
The missing piece (peace)
The cruel sword
Someday the sweet release

For you have promises to keep and a journey
before you sleep
The water is deep
But He is deeper

The Heart Murmur

The doctor used his stethoscope
And sadly shook his head and said
It sounds as if there is no hope
It sounds as if you have a heart murmur
I've consulted with my colleagues and we concur
We don't know what it is saying
Perhaps the angels praying
Seems as if it might be congenital
Never had a chance to fill
A part of it is still
Perhaps it is a hole in the heart
Although we know it stops and starts
Once again he listened carefully and said
It is something we cannot see
What we do know is that it is an injury
We could try a replacement part for your heart
But the kind you need...There is no part
We are not skilled at what was "killed"
We are in no position
You will need to consult the "great physician"
We do not know what to do
You will have to
Self-repair
It is up to you

The Broken

Where do the broken go to die?
Does anyone hear their hopeless cry
It must be you
It must be I
Haunted eyes
Lost in paradise
Beaten by life
And all of its strife
Looking for someone to care
Someone to share
Hopeless and hard to bear
Life is not fair
Where is the justice?
Is it just hit or miss?
We cannot fathom why
Born to cry
Born to die
We should
Be born
To fly

Bird of Paradise

The bird of paradise flies
But with tears in her eyes
She is usually in disguise
It is no surprise
It has always been that way
Until she sees the day
When she can smile
After journeying so many a trial
So many a mile
The memories fly past
In single file
She needs to rest awhile
She searches for a safe place
Those tears to erase
A soft place to land
For a welcoming hand
She never had a nest
A place to rest
It seems as though life has continuously been
A painful test
No one and nothing could prevent her from flying
Even though at times

Her spirit
Came near to dying
No one could capture her
Because
She would remember
Stay vigilant and strong
Live on
Don't let anyone steal
Your joy and song
Live on

Mandolins

Violin strings
Moonbeams on flying wings
Fuzzy caterpillars with their rolling little walk
An intimate quiet little talk
Music—the heart of the soul
Makes me whole
Flaming sunsets
Delicate dawn
Love lies on
The orchestra swells
Its story soon to tell
The dance
Pure romance
Take that chance
A softly falling rain
To gentle away the pain
To live
And love
Again

The Triumph of Endurance

I mourn that tender sensitive, passionate child
Who had no choice but to endure a "ride" so wild
I mourn the young bride
Whose hopes and dreams for love were dashed
inside
I mourn for the woman who was able to see
The rainbow through the hurricane
Who could still look up
In spite of all the pain
Who triumphed while anguishing
To help the suffering
Who felt nigh unto perishing
I mourn for all that never was
Which sometimes gives me pause
I mourn for those who mourn
Whose lives were sad and torn
For those who were never born
But
I celebrate
The woman who spoke out loud
The woman who never
Bowed

A Cloud

A cloud of witnesses
Angels blowing kisses
Spring rain
To come to life again
Returning what the locusts had eaten
For you were never beaten
In beautiful Fall which you anticipate every year
It will be sunny and cool and clear
And you will feel my presence near
You have never had anything to fear
You can rejoice
I have heard your song and voice
Now
Others will
Be at
Peace
Be still

Safe At Rest
Love from the Angels

Close your eyes and slumber deep
The rest of innocence
You now sleep
Our vigil we eternally keep
We stand guard
Over your life so hard
We smile upon you
For you are new
A wounded healer and over comer
We are proud of her
The precious journey of the few
To use the nightmare
To journey
Into love and care
Others journeys and pain to bear
For "joy cometh in the morning"
For you that is past and over (mourning)
The dark is past
At last
Your heart can begin to sing
Carillons of hope and joy
Without alloy

To the Wounded

Touch their hearts
Pull out those fiery darts
Touch the souls
Of lives which seem to be out of their control
Lift them from their deep dark hole
Raise them up from deep despair
They need someone to care
Let them see a glimpse
Of Me
Point out the son (sun)
Let them know they've just begun
Lead them from dark night
Into new vision and sight
"You've done it unto the least of these
You've done it unto me"
Be the miracle
And let them see
They can be free
Indeed
The best is yet to be
The compassion of our love to others bring
The truth rings out chimes of hope and love

We watch you from above
Continue to do what we have sent you to do
And in doing so wherever you go
Seeds of love you will be able to sow
If you listen carefully
You will hear us (angels) whisper low
Now...go
Listen...for this is your mission
Give to others who feel they have no hope
Who live in despair
Thinking that no one could ever care
Lift up the broken
With kindness gently spoken
Tenderly say
How may I help you today
And
Let me pray
I know you will be okay

The Spirit of Eiderdown

As soft as eiderdown
With not the slightest sound
As tender as the brush of a butterfly
A newborn's sleepy sigh
His spirit draweth nigh
He hears your painful cry
The dragonfly against the velvet rose
He knows you the way no one else knows
Alights with tenderness
The glow of spiritness
I can never fail
The thorns cannot impale
Upon my own
Because you are the flower
Which I have grown
If you can take my nail-scarred hand
I will lead you to the promised land
I will love you until the day you die
For I have ever loved you and heard your cry
I have given you the wings to fly
I will see you in the bye and bye
For now it is time to live

Give as much of Me as you can give
Live and laugh and dance and love
I will be watching and smiling from above
Love one another as I have loved you
Drink from the petals
The sunrise dew
I gave you my spirit
Peace, let others see and hear it
Peace, let others see and cheer it
You my mirror image can be
When people see you they should see Me
So until that day
When I whisper—away
Be my eyes and ears
To those who suffer
Be there
To wipe away their tears

The Chimes

It chimes midnight in the valley of the soul
I feel someone tried my joy to steal
I see no lights on the hills and mountains
Only darkness flowing as fountains
Walking and journeying through the pain
Through sheets of drenching rain
I walk
Into myself again
No one can ever steal my joy or smile
And so
I walk another mile

Flying

Like all of the butterflies and birds of the sky
I always knew that I
Was meant to fly
To listen to my heart
The quiet moments
Where the music starts
Never to walk...but to dance
So all will know
Angels walk and dance and stand
Close beside me
Guiding me
And when I fly
The current of their wings uplifting me
Reaching down from infinite eternal space
And sky
They sing and bring to me
We knew it all along
You have found your way
Your story is in your song
You have found your voice
Oh grateful heart
Rejoice

The Grateful Heart

I've always had a grateful hart
For everything I have had
Right from the start
No expectations from life
No silver spoon or silver knife
Able to make my way out into the world
No matter what obstacles at me were hurled
No, no silver spoon
Knowing that on the other side of the moon
There was daylight somewhere
That I could bear whatever I needed to bear
My faith has never let me down
I was wearing an invisible crown
Of royalty
Because of Him, able to be what I needed to be
It was all for a reason
Pain knows no season
A wounded healer and over comer
Eternal summer
A born optimist
By this blessed and kissed
The privilege of helping those in pain

Some of the wounded
Unable to cope ever again
The wealth of knowledge
Not learned in a college
Knowing the right things to say
Allowing for a brighter day
My feet are planted exactly where they are meant
to be
On a path where at the end I will see
The panorama of everything
My grateful heart
Has always been born
To sing

This Music

Overwhelms my soul
Emotions not under my control
A tidal wave
Drowns me in its beauty
Speaking loveliness to me
You have always been free
Lifts me to the stars
Then slams me down so far
I cannot rise
While hearing paradise
Passion and pain
A driving rain
So intense I cannot breathe
And yet
I cannot leave
Imprisoned by its spell
What is the message it is trying to tell
Strings tenderly weeping
Searching
Seeking
The dying, the grieving
The flute so sensitive and sad

For humanity and a life they have never had
Wanting to fling myself to the floor
Unbearable, unshareable
I cannot listen anymore
Exquisite and still
I must visit it
Revisit the pain
To come to life again
Love is patient, Love is kind"
Love is blind
Angels
Speaking, weeping, talking
Teaching, Seeking
A drenching waterfall
I hear its call
Saying that
Although the heart may shatter
Love
Is all that matters

Magical Trip

I am a child of (Heaven) Maine
A child of the wind and rain
A child sometimes
Of unending pain
Standing on the prow of a Viking ship
An ancient magical trip
The spirit of the Norsemen
The past of what has been
The blood singing in my veins
Experiencing humanity's awesome pain
Facing the storm and gale
A faith which never seems to fail
My countenance into the wind and waves
Never to bend and never to cave
Working and hoping to rescue and save
The sea-spray drenching me
But I will always be able to see
Humanity's pain
Right in front of me
Yes
A child of the storm
Mourning for all which has never been born

Willing to march into hell for a heavenly cause
Never seeming to give a pause
My life will always be worth living
Must continue to always be giving
The woman on the prow of the Viking ship
Stands fast without ever a slip
Stoic, intense and inwardly battered
Even though the heart was shattered
The rhythm of life
Humming, thrumming
Waiting once more
A song to sing
Always want to keep my lamp all glowing and lit
To be a beacon of hope for others
Since we are all our sisters, our brothers
When you see the storm out on the ocean
You can know that is where I have been
I can see the rainbow in a hurricane
The beauty of wildflowers
In a muddy, forgotten lane
I see paradise
I see homecoming when I see Maine
The Hope...The Child

A child of passion and joie de vivre
A child of Eve
I can see potential
In rains torrential
And
The light in the darkest velvet night
In deepest silent Winter
I can see Spring
When all around
Nothing seems as if it will ever sing
We should live as if we are dying
Because
We are

The Hope...The Child

A child of passion and joie de vivre
A child of Eve
I can see potential
In rains torrential
And
The light in the darkest velvet night
In deepest silent Winter
I can see Spring
When all around
Nothing seems as if it will ever sing
We should live as if we are dying
Because
We are

In My Sister's Pain
(Dedicated to All Who Have Been Abused)
A "Conversation" Between an Abused Woman
and Her Friend Who Doesn't Understand

Thirty-one years of abuse (me)
The unabused seem so all obtuse
I escaped
You were being raped
I was able to stand up
While your minds so cruelly struggled to escape
Minds tortured, reformed and shaped
Into something unrecognizable
I was fortunate to be strong
While you were told everything you did was wrong
Thousands of you will die this year
How long will this exist
How many are living in this nightmare of fear
No way to measure this here
The cruelest thing anyone can ever say
Why don't you just leave?
Beaten down
I don't know
Perhaps I have no place to go

I have no job skills
You could try if you wanted to
Plenty of jobs to be filled
He has threatened to murder me
You worry for nothing, can't you see
He has threatened to take my children away
Oh, stop complaining all day
He beats me day and night
If you wanted to you could fight
He said if I told
Why can't you be like me..so bold
He would throw me out into the cold
I have no friends, he's driven them all away
Oh, come on, let's do lunch, we'll make it a day
Just for us girls, I've been wanting some new pearls
Just for us, what is the fuss
I wear long sleeves in the Summer
Wow, that must be such a bummer
The bruise on my eye is always
I walked into a door
Now you are beginning to bore
My children are afraid
Well, it is your bed you have made
I would never put up with that I know
Criticism..blaming the victim

Quiet
Spoken so cruel and low
My family is afraid to come to my house
I cannot understand why you are such a mouse
I have given up hope
Oh, you seem like you cope
He ripped the phone out of the wall
I have no way to make a call
Well, just go to a phone. a quick trip to the mall
I have no car
It's good exercise, it cannot be far
He rapes me day and night
How can you let this happen...If I were you I would
put up a furious fight
What is happening to my mind
Gee, and he seems so kind
He twisted my arm
All I see is a boyish charm
He chokes me into unconsciousness
You look okay to me. I don't see any stress
He bit my breasts and also my arm
I can only see his charm
(Timidly) Could I borrow a few dollars
Usually that would be cool
But I have to pay for that new pool

But any other time just give me a call
I've been to the hospital so many times
You look okay to me, I don't see the crime
My mind feels like it is going insane
What is that car doing in my lane
I am afraid to call the police
Well, just do it...I have shopping to do
All this complaining, I wish it would cease
What is happening to me
Well, don't worry
It will all get better, just wait and see
No one understands or seems to care
I've got an appointment, have to color my hair
What would you do in my place
I would just get in his face
My children are hungry and he uses cocaine
I try to keep all of us sane
Well gotta run and it has been fun
Let me know if there is something I can do
Gosh, I thought that by talking to you
It seems I have trusted the wrong person
Well, this is nothing new
Wonder when he is coming home
I'd better hurry and clean the house and get the
dishes done

Just time to get the supper on
So he won't know
That I have been gone
I hope he doesn't take out that gun
Sitting there slowly, silently cleaning it
He knows that I will not run
He calls me names
Plays mind games
Emotional abuse destroys the soul
Shatters the mind
Total annihilation
Murder of the spirit and soul
The abusers objective...total control
He screams obscenities and hides the keys
Pummels me to my knees
He says it is only to tease
I try to please
I know I am worthless (he says so) and no good
I wish I could die
But I have no courage for that
I am only just occasionally
Able to cry
Sometimes he brings me flowers ("honeymoon
phase")
Then after a few hours my mind is in a maze

Screams at me
You are so stupid
No one would ever want you
I know that is true
Without him what would I do
I'd be better off dead
He pushes me onto the bed
I have to do what he has said
My children have to be fed
(One in three women are being abused)
Systematically brainwashed and accused
(From me)
I cry and mourn and bleed for you
But that is not enough
I have to get your story out
It is what I am meant to do
Thirty-one years...a waterfall of tears
Living in sadness and hopeless fears
Anytime one of you dear sisters leaves
I celebrate you
But there is so much more to do
Wake up, America!
The time is way past
How many more have to die
Until you hear their dying cry

Why don't you just leave
How that causes my heart to grieve
I feel such fury
Who made the ignorant anyone's judge or jury
Blame and shame
The ignorant's game
Excuses for not knowing
Unbelievably lame
What will it take
The Universe to shake
(Back to the conversation)
My children need me
I am all that they have
My bruises are aching, but I have run out of salve
From the beating last night
My eyes are bruised
I feel so beaten down and confused
I hope I won't lose my sight
This is a crime against humanity
No one wants to know or see
There is no one who can understand
No one to reach out and touch my tired hand
This is a horror in our land
Together we must band
It must not go hidden anymore

Unbar that door
We must bring this nightmare out
If I have to I will scream and shout
I will get it out
When I die, if I go to hell
How will I know
How will I tell
Oh, I know
I will recognize it right away
Just get out of bed and start another nightmare
day
"When you blame me, you shame me,and keep me
silent"
Silent no more
We must fling open that door

The Forgotten

Just before the thunder rolls
Just before the church bell tolls
The sense of anticipation quietly steals
Over a mind which has needed to heal
The moment before the crescendo
While the music is still so sweet and low
In the eye of the hurricane

I walked through all of their pain
The moment before someone leaps into space
Standing up to their evil face to face
The moment of a newborn's cry
I could not cry
I did not die
Sometimes the escape of a worn-out sigh
The quietude of a peaceful painting
I was not born for fear or fainting
Eyes which meet across a room
Not for me their gloom and doom
The warming touch of a cherished friend
My soul and will not be theirs to bend
A child's first word
I will be heard
An old couple quietly rocking on a porch
I can be the torch

For the abused so hopeless and confused
Who believe they have no choice
No voice
If I can help just one
It will be done
For they are hungry, but not for bread
In silence they are bleeding
In pain they so long are pleading

The darkness is surrounding me
Why is it that no one cares to see
Left alone is all I will ever be
I can see no light
I must give up this hopeless fight
Eternal night
I keep looking at those pills
I keep fighting it, my mind so ill
Please
Someone help me
My soul and heart are chilled
To sleep, escape the pain
Which never seems to stop and visits me
Again, again, again

Why is no one there
To ease my deep despair
Why haven't I heard from you, oh God

Do you hear me
Those others say, "just pray"
I don't want to live, can't fight another day
The razor is in my hand
How much of this should I be able to stand
The abuser(s) tell me the fault is mine
Tomorrow they say
The sun will shine

I may not see it
Just want to quit
I haven't the strength to shout
Somebody...anybody
The all encompassing sadness
For you the sun may shine tomorrow
For me there is only this unending sorrow
My wounded soul and mindlessness
Out of control I must confess
Ocean waves are crashing
While before my eyes my life is flashing
The Universe holds its breath
To see what I will do
The choice for life or death
I wait for help
Will you just ignore the soul which is dying

Just beyond your open door

The darkness is closing in
What was my sin
It enfolds me in its alluring charm
It beckons me—I mean no harm
So soon it could be over
Just lie down and do not stir
The glimmer of hope others can see
Is not for someone like me

With ease I can whisk you far away
There will be a better day
Will you go with me or
Shall I wait to see
If you will cope
Without someone to care
Someone to give you hope
If no one comes to save your life
I hold the answer
With a knife
Or
Over there
A chair
A rope to end your despair
A tragedy
No one heard
And didn't care

The Chrysalis

To bear the unbearable
To share the unshearable
To live with ones own company
With the future unknown
Unable to see
The struggle to reach the sun
While feeling so undone
Like a flower reaching to bloom
Would like to return to the womb
Tears come unbidden
From the world hidden
The ache of the heart
Apart
To heal
All the feelings one must feel
An angel whispers in my ear
There is nothing you have to fear
We are always here
We are always near
Your heart has songs to sing
Messages of hope to others bring
This is not the end

But the beginning
Like the chrysalis
Anticipating bliss
The breath of life
That "kiss"
Your wings are gently fanning
Resting, thinking, healing, planning
For a life you have never had
Not ever what you wanted, sad
Liftoff time is near
If you listen to our music
You will hear
The magic
Loud and clear
Lift up your eyes
And claim the prize
Now sing
Now dance
Now fly
The clouds await to meet you
In the sky
Yes
That is how high

The Cathedral of the Soul

Needing to be whole
Singing songs of hope and love
Hearing angels from above
Pressing forward into life each day
Trying not to look back
For
You are not going that way
There resides the slightest quiver
The heart is moved
The body shivers
The need to grieve
The need to leave
Let go of broken promises
Betrayals of those kisses
The hope of things to come
For now
A sense undone
The sense of loneliness
Of onliness
Barbed wire
A heart wrapped in fire
Piano wire

Reverberates
Anticipates
Lying still
Waiting for that touch to fill
The magic touch
To come to life
And sing
Beauty to others bring
And Life
To a dying thing
Breath taken away
By the body's consuming desire
The passion and need
A soul to bleed
One day the chains will fall
I can say I am freed
Tears mix with rain
Bowed by the pain
Hard to breathe
I cannot stay and I cannot leave
Still on the journey, the walk with grief
A flower pushes through the dark and dirt
Struggling against the hurt
Spring and growing things
Spring and blossoming rings

Spring and a robin sings
All nature commands
New life and birth
Things becoming new
That is what (we) I have to do

The Fatherless Child

I never knew my father
Only had a mother
I wonder what he thought about me
Did he wonder who would she be
Did he ever
Perhaps never
Rock me in his arms
Enjoy my baby charms
Sing a lullaby
Or comfort a little cry
Play and jiggle me
Hold me on his knee
Throw me gently into the air
Caress my sun-warmed hair
Kiss my cheek and gently speak
Give me a bath
Smile upon hearing me laugh
Hold my hand
Did I play in the sand
Watch me creep
Rock me to sleep
Love me so deep

Ruffle my hair
Gaze upon my sleeping face
Hold me close
Chase away a scary "ghost"
Think that I might be a princess
Think that I might be special and maybe famous
Listen to me breathe
Upon leaving, did he grieve
Stroll me in a carriage
Think about a marriage
Put me on a sled
Hold a spoon so I would be fed
Watch me toddle
Give me a bottle
Dance with me all joyfully
Catch me when I would fall
Why wasn't he there at all
Did I grasp his finger
Did he hold his breath in wonder
Did he let his heart linger
Over my innocent face
In my innocent place
Did he think what I might have to face
Pick me up and hold my cup
So little hands could drink

Did he ever think
His only thought was for a drink
Hold his breath while I took a step
Did he count my toes and kiss my little nose
Hold me up to the sky
So I could watch a butterfly
Breezily flutter by
Did he squeeze me in delight
Was he gentle with my fright
Hold a buttercup under my chin
To see if it reflected the mood I was in
Blow some bubbles
Tell me, those are your troubles
Blow on my tummy
Did I think it was funny
Smile at my toothless grin
Burst with pride and feel like a king
Feel such joy
Watching me play with a toy
Hold a flower to my nose
Tell me that it was like me...a rose
Breathe and drink in my baby fragrance
Play peek-a-boo and say
I love you
Feel so proud and say it out loud

Look at those huge brown eyes
Someone will love her and bring her paradise
Did he dress me, cherish me
Put little arms and legs into pajamas for bed
Make sure that I had been fed
Did he play "This Little Piggy" with my toes
Nobody knows
Sit with me when I was sick
Try to figure out what made me tick
I don't think so
I never grieved over what I never had
Never thought of him as dad
He disappeared and as I feared
Why no father...into my life was seared
I have no memory
Of what he was like with me
What loss and grief
He stole away
Forever like a thief
The loss, anguish and fear
All written here
The loss, so very dear
That was my first experience with
Goodbye
I never got to ask him

Why
All of life has been about goodbye
Each time I wonder why
There are some things which should never be
God should change
Sad history

The Hour

My heart is torn apart
Lies as
A stone
Pain on pain
Bone on bone
The heart still beats
But not by choice
Listening to a quiet voice
Still stand with courage in the heart
While you and love
Remain apart
Weeping in your sleep
Dreaming dreams so deep
A silent vigil of the soul
Whispers
We still keep
The pathway steep
A craggy knoll
The hands of the timepiece read
The hour
Is
Half-past midnight
In the valley of the soul

Exquisite Speaking Violins

An instrument of pain
A drenching rain
Which sobs its own refrain
An instrument of love
Cooing softer than any dove
To lie down again
Be free from pain
One can almost feel insane
An instrument of mankind's infinite passion and
hope
So a dying wounded soul can cope
Can you hear it speak
The power of the climax peak
The crescendo wild
As if a frantic child
An instrument of love
Haunting, calling angels from above
Can you hear its whisper soft and low
Going where no others go
Follow me for I must go
To memories and hope
Where only angels sow

And where the ocean flows
And I am freed
No harps again, for they will never mend
Music therapy
The violin speaks to me
I will be your constant friend
I will never go away, there will be no end
I will soothe your soul and brow
If you just bend to me just now
The beauty of the world
When I commence to sing
Shown to you with miracles unfurled
All holy and so pure
Like you
I do endure
Heaven sounds like this
An angel kiss
Softer than the angel's wing
Such joy to heartache I always bring
If heaven feels like this
I will have my wish
Sometimes unbearable
The soul to fill
Unutterable to the human voice
One does rejoice

Because to me
It sounds like praying
Without words
One cannot speak
It must be heard
For only those who love
Can hear the sounds
Cascading
Pouring down from up above
Only those who love can feel
How it is sweet and real
Sobs of passion
Soaring, pouring out
While your eyes repose in ecstasy
But you still can see
For this is the way it was meant to be
Laugh and cry and dance and shout
The violin can only bring that out
But you must open up
Drink from the music
As if from a silver cup
It will speak to you
Like nothing else you ever knew
And will renew
Your very soul, its only goal

As finest gold
Ancient beauty
As in days of old
Only those who love
Can hear its message
Streaming down from up above
Only those who've cried and "died"
Can hear its message
Awake and come inside
They with such poverty of mind and spirit
Can never hear it
The land of the violin
Where life begins anew...again
Bringing thoughts of
Fragrant flowers
Sleepy bowers
Whiling away the untold hours
Pansies with their pretty faces
Queen Anne's flowers with their filigreed laces
Lightening bugs
Fantasies and dreams
The north star winking
To magical moonbeams
Tiny kittens purring
Batting their velvet mittens

Little old ladies and drowsy babies
Wishes turning into okays and maybes
Dragonflies and lullabies
Mysterious fog and moonlit skies
Ladybugs and tight, hard hugs
A stringed symphony
A million voices singing the "Hallelujah Chorus"
Deep, dark chocolate in creamy mugs
Robert Mondavi wine
Faces that beam and shine
God
The Divine
A quiet mood
Music—as soul food
A passionate kiss
Total bliss
Maine (Heaven) in gorgeous Fall
I hear her call
A majestic waterfall
The whippoorwill's sweetest call
I am not on earth at all
Fairy wings
Silvery, shiny things
Snowflakes falling slowly
As if in a water globe

Gently sifting
Just as drifting
A forest dark and quiet
Oh weep and mourn
While beauty is being born
Evergreens soughing
Homeward at dusk, birds are flying
I rise
To claim the prize
Exquisite rapture
Nothing else can ever capture
Beauty and elegance and poetry
Is who I want to be
As if caught by a raging storm
Overwhelmed and swept away
Flying in a lightening cloud
When night has turned to day
Profound
Unable to utter a sound
The pain is real
The notes they steal
Me far away
To another time and day
Where the only rule
Is that you must play

In another universe
Oh
Sing that powerful verse
I will rehearse
The ecstasy
And dance the melody
You bring to me
Where only those
Who have eyes to see
The completed me
Totally free
The land of violin
If you can hear its message
Where life begins again
I weave such magic
Into lives so tragic
I calm the soul
For those who feel
They've lost control
I tenderly minister and weep
To wake you from your sleep
I am here to cheer
Give voice to fear
If I have the chance
I will see you dance

I speak and moan
For those alone
I wrap your fears in light
To those
Who have lost
Their sight

Mourning

I mourn that tender sensitive, passionate child
Who had no choice but to endure a "ride" (abuse)
so wild
I mourn the young bride
Whose hopes and dreams for love
Were dashed inside
I mourn for the child unborn
The husband who didn't allow me to mourn
I mourn for the woman who was able to see
The rainbow through the hurricane
Who could still look up
In spite of all the pain
Who triumphed while anguishing
To help the suffering who felt
Nigh unto perishing
I mourn for all that never was
Which sometimes gives me pause
I mourn for those who mourn
Whose lives were torn
But
I celebrate
The woman who spoke up out loud
The woman
Who never bowed

Three Tears

Three tears slipped so silently
Down my soul
Unbidden
Deep
Hidden
Without a sound
Deep
Profound
Sometimes the mind forgets to cry
The spirit's constant vigil
Reminds it
Why

The Id

The Inner bratty kid
Ahhhh, yes the infamous Id
I'd like to blow off the lid
I would like to scream and shout
Let it all hang out
Have a monumental temper tantrum
Pound on a big steel drum
It is not fair
And I do not care
I feel like I could break a chair
This is just too much to bear
I want what I want right now
I want to have it and I don't care how
So give it to me right nor or I will hold my breath
To my very death
I would like to pound on the floor
Break down a door
And what is more
It's violence I abhor
I want it it is mine
I am so out of line
I guess it is a sign
I try so hard to behave divine

I need to behave
My temper save
All out of control screaming loud and wild
Gimmee-Gimmee
Can't you see
It belongs to me
Don't think you can ever put me over your knee
I was always told I was so selfish so they say
If you are going to do the time
You might as well do the crime
You know
So now I am allowing my temper to just let go
Whatever it wants to do
So what are you going to do
I am going to go out and play
I refuse to even tie my shoes
I will make you pay
For not giving me my way
You will be sorry some day
I am going to blow my nose
On the garden hose
I am going to swear
I don't really care
Just how much
Nobody knows

I am going to stick out my tongue
Watch you get all undone
Stick my fingers in my ears
Sneak one of dad's favorite beers
Yell and ruin dad's golf putts
In supermarket lines
Take lots of cuts
I think groanups (not a misspelling)
Should have to drink from sippy cups
Going to swing the cat
And spin him around
See what he does
When he hits the ground
If he makes any sound
Steal a bike
That is what I would like
Cross my eyes and make a face
The computer hardrive I will erase
I am such a case
We'll see who pays their dues
I've left enough wreckage and so many clues
I won't ever again eat my broccoli
And no one and nothing can ever make me
I am running away from home
I will never again

Use a brush or a comb
I will grab dad's beer and blow off the foam
Matter of fact
I am never going to eat again
I will be living with the wolves in their den
They will treat me better than you do
I know they won't care when I come or go
I am going to eat like the pigs in a trough
Won't put my hands over my mouth when I sneeze
or cough
I will never take a bath
When people are shocked at how I look
I will just laugh
I will be a wild little thing
The wolves will give me what I want
Little treats to them
I will bring
I am such a case
Who can keep up the pace
You cannot spank me
You cannot even catch me
You will be sorry someday
You will wish I had never left and gone away

Cabin in the Woods

Winter skies
Lullabies
Sleepy kitten sighs
Freshly fallen snow
Against a cozy cabin lies
Snowflakes and stars
Softly humming
Spanish guitars
Moons and stars
Venus and Mars
Reality blurs
Against the softly painted firs
Magic and light
Imagination takes flight
Mesmerized by beauty
In my sight
Beauty in the night
I look up to see a shooting star
The tail is as long as a kite
The night ends perfectly

The wish I made
So I could see
When a dream dies
An angel cries
An angel flies
To comfort the soul
Whose dream
Was never realized

Flying

Like all of the butterflies and birds of the sky
I always knew
That I was meant to fly
To listen to my heart
The quiet moments
Where the music starts
Never to walk
Always to dance
So all will know
Angels walk and dance and stand beside me
Guiding me
And when I fly
Their wings uplifting me
Reaching down from infinite, eternal space
They sing and bring to me
We knew all along
You've found your way
Your story is in your song
You've found your way oh grateful heart
Rejoice

God's Abacus

Tiny little birds
Singers without words
Lined upon a telephone wire
Looking like an abacus
Moving to and fro
Ruffling feathers with a fuss
Little dots here and there
Leaving little spaces bare
Riders in the sky
Coming and going
Their flight so high
Sliding back and forth
Counting blessings twice
Chirping love and bird advice
Counting their little families
Loving to play and tease
Melodies in the breeze
We'll count ourselves blessed
And be on our way
Come back on the morrow
To live and sing and play

Ghost Child to Triumph

I've mourned the child
That never was
The reason I've helped
Is for a cause
Once called a "fairy-child' 'tis true
Everything now
Becoming new
Unknown, unheard by anyone
The long, long search
For a place in the sun
Some of that child remains today
She now speaks up in a big, big way
She has learned that now
It is time to fly
Upon a precipice
Away up high
A butterfly with wings of gold
Shimmering in the sunlight
Now out of the cold
What happens to her is now
Is up to me
She has done her work
Now she is
Free